A broken line at midnight

By: Ayaana Noman

To my dad, who encouraged me to finish this book

To my Mom, who told me to stop stressing over nothing

To my friend, you know who you are

To all the people who question why they chose to open this book

To you...

Life is sad
That's why I'm mad.

-My mother

Table of contents:

Happily ever after
The plague
The man in the mirror
The "truth" of your words
Memory loss
The man in my dreams
The clock
The wall
Books: The new reality!
The garbage-filled city
The truth of reality
Their "heartwarming" messages
Good memories
The truth of love
The flood of denial
Island of doom
Society's never happy, But are you?
Shipwreck of 12
Take off
Abandonded sky
Choose wisely
Bricks of diamonds
The shallow yard
Drowning of the lover

Brain decay
Everything with nothing
Mocking mirror
He's coming back?
Intricacies of a simple thing
The lies we tell ourselves
The misunderstood
The beauty of the terror
Galaxy of hope
Complexity of life
The irreversible
Numbered days
Inhuman v. Human
Blood pumping
½ of a heart
Why not?
It's too early
Tough planet
Duality of a face
Inevitable experience
You are still operating
Look in the mirror
Foreground middle ground background
Monsters under our bed
2% remaining

A broken line at midnight

Alone in his house
A man stood
Holding a telephone in his bare hands
Covered in dust
With his eyes wide open
With rivers and clouds
Tearing them apart

The man stood
All night
Till the clock hit 12
Waiting for a single sentence
Only to have realized that the line
Had been cut

Ode to the vampire

My calm sweet gorgeous vampire
Oh how you inspire me to write
Oh how I hate when others
Run scream and hide
From your sight
Shielding their hearts from your prying eyes
You invade my mind day and night
Showing up in my dreams and promising
not to bite

My calm sweet vampire
Let me compare you to a mercenary
Only much more scary and terrifying
Your sharp blood white teeth
Cooler than the ice bites through the breeze
of January
Grazing over my skin
Promising you won't bite

My calm vampire
Your touch is cold to the core
Enlightening goosebumps on my skin
As if I'm the prey you eat on a cool night

In which you break your promise
While the wind howls the scent of iron
In which runs down my skin

My vampire
Oh how you truly inspire me to write
But unfortunately, my hands are too tied
In the bloody mess, you created with my
heart on this cool winter night

A true hero

What does it mean to be a hero?
It doesn't mean to be powerful
To be loved by all
To have abilities others cannot possess
To be a sorcerer
To have your own comic
To be beautiful or pretty
It means to be beautiful on the inside
To stick up for the little
To choose kindness every day as you get out
of bed
To be the best man woman and person you
can be
To do the unseen actions of kindness
You don't have to be big and strong to be a
hero
You don't need to be buff
Or be able to lift a thousand pounds
You just need a beautiful heart
Filled with love and joy
Not somber and gray filled with hurricanes
of sadness

To be a hero you need a passion for the
things people chose to ignore.
The things people overlook
Anyone can be a hero
You just need to try
You don't need a pretty sword or weapon
You don't need killer fighting skills
You don't have to be rich and famous
You don't have to be an actor or actress
You don't even have to do anything amazing
A true hero does the small actions from the
bottom of their heart
Not from the top of a tower
Or at a desk filled with millionaires
To be a hero you must evolve
Love
Express
You must not
Hate
Be angry
Rude
Think of yourself above others
A true hero wouldn't be so selfish
Or self-centered
To be a hero

You must share kindness and gratitude with
others
On your own
To be a hero you must choose your actions
not have someone tell you
It must come from the bottom of your heart
Tall or short
Big or small
Weak or strong
We all can be heroes
Every day when we get up we have a choice
And if we all chose the right one then we all
can be true heroes
Yet the people in this world don't
They chose to ignore the calling on the right
side of the bed
They chose to be selfish and mean
Hurtful and filled with hatred
And those who do choose the right path are
ridiculed and shamed by those who don't
Those who choose the right path are
embarrassed and unhappy by the negativity
of those who don't
Those who chose not to be heroes every day
cause the true heroes to stray from the path

Forcing them to conform and become
somebody they don't want to be.
We all could be heroes in this world
Make it a better place
Filled with love and joy
Instead of black somber fill with the heart of
the devil
Which is why I ask myself day and night
Why I ponder
Why I question

What does it truly mean to be a hero?

The tidal wave

Atychiphobia:
The fear of failure
The fear of failure can wash over you like a
tidal wave
The fear of failure follows you wherever
you go whether you walk or run
You can't run from the great tidal wave of
failure
Whenever the great tide of fear washes over
you
You can feel your throat closing twisting
turning and choking you up on saltwater like
a hurricane
Whenever you stare into the abyss of your
paper or screen looking at the big bold mark
that is anything but good
You can feel your hands start to shake and
feel a sudden urge of panic rush through
your entire body
Sending fireworks off in your stomach
The only thoughts that run through your
mind are telling you that you're worthless

That you're bad at everything you've ever
done and managed to complete in life
Your head keeps screaming and yelling at
you that you've failed and all you want to do
is run away from your own body and swim
out of the great tidal wave of failure
Yet at your own demise, you can't get out
and hit rock bottom
Of the ocean floor

Suck it up

Note: Do not read if stressed…..

Essay due at *8:16 P.M*
But it's already *8:15 P.M*
And I haven't even started

I have work *Tomorrow*
So I have to get up at *5:00 A.M*
But it's already *4:00 A.M* and I haven't got a
drop of sleep yet

I have school *Tomorrow*
Biology **TEST** *Calculus* **TEST** *Spanish*
TEST *Chemistry* **TEST** *Physics* **TEST**
History **TEST** *Economics* **TEST**
All *next week*
I have to get good grades or I won't *pass*
If I don't get good grades my parents will be
mad
If I *fail* I have to retake the class

I have to go to work or else how will I
survive

How will I *feed* my kids myself my parents
and everyone else?

I have to drink water
I have to eat
I have to go to the store
Clean my clothes
Pay my bills
Go to the doctor
Go to the gym
Go to work
Go to college
All by *next week*
Otherwise, I won't have a *life*

I have bills due by *tomorrow* or else I will
be *evicted*
And I won't have a home

I have to clean my clothes or I won't have
anything to *wear*

I have to eat and drink unless I want to
perish

I have to do all these things to *live*

Every single day
I worry and stress I won't make it on time
That I won't be able to survive
Yet I keep going
I stress for no reason yet everything ends up
going just fine
Even if I fail and fail
Life still goes on
Life won't wait for you to catch up
For you to get over your stress
Every day you stress about things that have
yet to happen
Yet life already has a plan for you
Your fate has already been decided
And you can't change that
So why stress about things that have already
been decided
Stress is a disease
One person talks about it and the next is
reminded
Stress is a part of life
Every day we breathe to live
Yet we aren't stressed to do it

Because we don't even think of it

In life, we will always be stressed
There will always be situations where stress
comes knocking on your front door
Yet we don't have to open that door
So suck it up
Life will always be stressful
Stress will always be on your shoulders
watching over you
But don't let the stress take over your being
Your happiness and emotions
Suck the stress up
Suck it up
And take a deep calm breath

Don't let stress take over your every thought
and emotion
Because stress will always be there
But no one said you had to give in
No one told you to exchange your happiness
for stress
Because that's just a poor deal

-A human who experiences the emotion of stress

Note: Maybe read if stressed.

Naturally defective

Quitter.
Failure.
Mistake.
Three words that can crush someone's day
Instantly causing them to fall off the crane
of doom and decay

Quitter.
A person who fails to complete things they
begin
A person who believes dreams and sweet
thoughts just for them not to be achieved

Failure
Someone who cannot accomplish their goals
Someone who believes they will be a star
just for them to fail at step number one

Mistake
A human not capable of completing the
simplest tasks with ease and efficiency
A human who cannot do their job right

People are ridiculed by these names
Called by them day and night
Just because they act as a true human being
Because they weren't perfect
But too bad no one in this world is perfect
To bad the people using these names are the
true quitters
The true failures and the true mistakes
Because they have the audacity to insult
instead of teach
Instead of helping others
Instead, they chose to hate
To ruin someone's day
Crush them off the crane of doom and decay
The ones being ridiculed aren't the problem
in this world
People that call others that are the true
problem
The true virus
The true disease
They're the ones that cause the mistakes
They cause the quitters
They cause the mistakes
Because no one is perfect
We are all human

With emotions
And feelings
We all feel
We all have a heart
Too bad some people's hearts are frozen
over
With jealousy and disease
Causing them to use these names
To express unwanted feelings of hate
To use their beautiful heart for negativity
Causing the beauty to turn to black charcoal
of decay spreading to others like a virus
causing quitter's failures and mistakes
They aren't perfect
No one is perfect
We are all humans
Imperfect
And shaped with clay
Built to embody and change
And to learn from our failures and mistakes
To prevent the actions of pain
And to prevent others from quitting their
dreams and goals
And driving others to succeed
To the path of goodness and great

Quitter.
Failure.
Mistake.
No.
We are all just humans trying to embrace.

The fool who pretends

Somedays you like to pretend
Pretend that you're okay
Say *"I'm fine."*
Over and over again
Those same two words
Ruining your life
Lies just rolling off your tongue
Day after day

Don't fool yourself
You know how you feel
That you don't know how to open up
without feeling judged
Feeling insecure
Words just begging and bleeding out of your
mouth at the wrong moment and time

People will eventually see your scars
They'll see right through your facade
Pretend doesn't last forever
They will see through your shield

People will see your hardships

But won't help
After all, it's your problem, not theirs
Little do they know the impact they can
make with a simple sentence

"Are you okay?"

That's why you stick to pretending
 to avoid anxiety and agony

"Yeah, I'm fine."

The curse of remorse

Regret
2 vowels 6 letters
Takes an instant to get off your tongue
Takes a flash to say
Regret is such a short word
And yet it spreads on forever

Regret
So perfect yet so imperfect
Regret can help you
Look back
But...
Regret can damage
drench you in fear and apprehension
Regret
Such a short utterance
And yet it stretches on forever

Regret is the former
Regret is so significant you can never get rid
of it
R-E-G-R-E-T
Such a short word

Yet it stretches on for eternity

Masks of pain

Everyone's the same
We all undergo emotions
We all put on our masks to enclose the
sickness and the pain
We all have a deep darkness beneath us
We all undergo pain
Every single day
Hitting us harder day by day
Yet we keep smiling and put on our masks
just to get through the day

Raindrops on a teary-eyed day

Tears are like raindrops on a cloudy day
Drip-drop…
Streams run down our face
Glimmering like crystals
Like a thousand diamonds on a sunny day

Tears are beautiful
But are there because of the pain
Tears show our hardships
Our emotions
Tears show the battles we have faced
Tears are like raindrops on a cloudy day
So beautiful yet so gray

The humorous cycle of life

Life is a cycle
A nearly never-ending cycle
We get-up
We fall asleep
We're all the same
Going through the same process day after
day
Day...after day..after day…
We're all the same
Till one day we all decay

The humanization of people

I fear that I don't deserve
That I don't deserve to be loved and
appreciated
I am empty and irritated
Selfish and mean
Angry and horrid
I can't help it
I try to stop the things that come out of my
mouth
But I'm always too late
Staying up at night wondering why I said
something
Why I did something
Why, why, why?
Thinking of what I did wrong
Thinking of why I did this and that
Instead of being someone else
But, I'm human too
Like everyone
I feel
I regret

But then I think back

To all the smiles and laughter I've earned
To all the times I've been useful
To all the friends that I've made
We all make mistakes
For I am still human too.

The question of the dead

I've been falling apart for all these years
Slowly and painfully
Ripping like a bandage
Yet you chose to notice
Only when I'm gone
You've noticed in pity
Not because you actually cared
Cause you didn't when I was here
Never about the muffled screams I made at
midnight
Never about the crying, I did when I was
alone
Never
Never at all
I had a question

"Why do we pity the dead, not the living."
 *"Why do we care when they're dead, not
alive?"*

And you failed to answer it
Instead, you went through with it.

The shadows of the night

They say happiness will find you even in the
darkest times
But it never does
Instead comes sadness
Disguised as happiness

They say sadness comes and goes
Yet a piece of it stays
Building up
Eating your thoughts alive
Till every shadow and shape
Is associated with darkness and pain
Every book and every poem
Relates to your saddest days

No one ever says that sadness will come
No one
Yet it always does
Knocking on my door
Living in the depths of my walls
Day and night
Begging to come in
And it always does

Creeping in on me through every crack and
hole
Consuming me slowly till there's nothing
left
Till it's just empty
Leaving me wondering
What I did to be alone
And when will it all end
"When?"

The reality of your footsteps

You walk away
Like everything is fine
But we all know
You're mad
You're mad at the world
Angry at the people
Displeased by the news
Mad at everything
You are so mad
That you're so sad
You're sad about how bad it is
So you channel it into anger
You're sad about the world
How it's almost destroyed
You're so upset about the people
How rude they are
How racist
How narcissistic
You're depressed about the news
How could this happen
You are so sad about everything
So much
That you turn your sadness into

Anger
Hurting yourself
And the
People around you
The people you love
The people you care about
Everyone.
"How could you?"

Tornado man

Imagine a tornado out of control
Sucking every sound second and noise right
off its feet
Seducing all the bad thoughts and dreams
Roping in all the bad feelings
Of jealousy
Distress
And chaos
And choosing to have a date
Right at your place
Inside your most powerful organ
That controls everything
From the way you think
To the way you breath

Hallucinations on the side of the road

On the road, I met a man
In his left hand, he was holding a bag of
cocaine
He said he felt a sense of euphoria
Said he craved to feel something
Wished to be something

Was willing to demolish his life
Just to feel again
Was willing to destroy himself just to feel
happy

He was willing to die for it
For a taste of something
D-I-E
A very bitter word in the existence of this
cruel world
How can we be this cruel to ourselves
Such pain and suffering

The man spoke as if he was warning me
Begging me not to follow his steps

Too bad, I was the one holding the drugs
instead.

45

It was all my subconscious
I was the man holding the drugs
On the road
I did my deed
I followed his steps
Because I was just hallucinating

Painfully unpainful

What's more painful and dangerous
Getting shot or a thought
A bullet is hard and smooth
Can kill in an instant
Pain being there for seconds
Till you close your eyes and sink to
subconsciousness
A thought will drag you down
Your entire life
Till you break down
Causing misery to be there
Day and night
Twenty four seven
To the grave
Both equally as dangerous
But a gun can kill you and a thought can
cause it

Now you think
What's really more painful and dangerous
Getting shot or a thought?

The little people

I'm terrified of the little voices
That scream in my head
The voices that scream
Day and night
The voices that drive me to hell and back
The voices that can end it all
I try to stop them from eating me up alive
Begging for mercy
But I'm so tired
So tired to fight back
I just want it to end
I just want to take a deep breath
And sink into freedom
But I can't
Because I will miss the subtle feelings of joy
I experience throughout my life

Popular girl

I wished to be famous and popular
I wished to feel something
Be something special
I wanted to be different
I wanted my voice to be known and heard
I wanted to be so successful that I never had
to introduce myself when I walk into a room
But here I am lying on my bed
Just wondering about my life
Wasting my days doing nothing
Just imagining what it would be like
To live a life like that
But then I think
How overwhelming It would be
How stressful
How irritating
Now I look back and think
How happy and appreciative I am of this life

Dreams of the universe

We all dream and hope for things to happen
But they never do
That's how life works
Life will never feel for you
Care for you
Pity you
Because life is a horrid thing
But sometimes you can find light and
prosperity
Even in the darkest times
But only if you strive

The future you

People say "Even in the far future
Never forget the you of right now"

What they're really trying to say is…
Never forget the memories you've made
Never forget the friends
The laughter
The smiles
And the joy
Never
Never forget the pain
The tears
Or the sadness
Cause one day you'll
Need it to find you again
To reflect
To learn
To destroy
To lead
And to be successful
Even in the far future
Could be thousands of days could be one
"Never forget the you

Of right now"

A brick of love

Love is a strong word
Like a wall of bricks
Strong and sturdy
Tall and wide
Big and bold
Red and gray
But it can still decay

Love may be strong
But only if built
right
Cause if not
It can break into thousands of pieces
Shatter just like your heart

Till there's nothing to put it back together

Love can be strong
If built right

Sadly nothing can ever be perfect
Nothing
Nothing at all.

Happily ever after

It's sad how we all grew up
Thinking we'd have a happy ending
How we thought all our lives
Would be perfect
Like a tv show
Living life
Without a care in the world
It's sad
How nowadays
People aren't waiting for there
Happy ending
They're just waiting
For it to get better
For it to end

The plague

What happened
What happened to the good old days
What happened to all the smiles
What happened?
What happened to us
Who have we become
We are like strangers
Like we've never met
Like we didn't exist to one another
We just faded
Faded away from each of our memories
Away from our smiles
And laughter
Our bond and friendship
Now we stand 5 ft apart
Like a tv show slowly zooming out on a
so-called broken character's life
Away from each other
like we're strangers
Like we're both the plague
Trying our best to avoid each other

The man in the mirror

I look in the mirror
I look hard and close
Squeeze my eyes till they feel like bleeding
I don't recognize myself
I don't remember looking like this
I don't know who I am
"Who am I ? "
Or who I'm looking back too
What happened to me
"what?"
When did this happen
" when?"

I'm unrecognizable

A whole new person

Like someone who cares too much about
what others think
Someone who stresses out
Over the littlest things
Someone that tries to be perfect

Someone who tries to please others instead
of themselves
"Am I not good enough..?"

My true embodiment is just a ghost of a
memory

I'm unrecognizable
Too busy caring about what others think
than myself
"Oh well...."

The "truth" of your words

There's a point in life
Where we're so tired and done with all the
lies you've said
All the hurt you've caused
That we pretend it doesn't exist.
Just for our sanity
Just for our health
For a moment of peace

Like a placebo
We put up a fake outside
In order to cope
Something fake
But with passion and belief

The problem is there are no side effects with
a placebo
Believing you'll get better
It's a good thing
However, Pretending it doesn't exist
Is a whole different case

People and medication

Two different things
Two different side effects
Placebos may not hurt you
But ignoring will
Cause one day you'll have to face it
Let reality smack you in the face
And withstand the pain

Memory loss

Memory is an important thing
A memory holds details
Details of your past and present
Details of the joy and sorrow

Memory is the evidence
Evidence to prove yourself
To prove you are not guilty
When one loses these thoughts
It can be simple to be framed
To be manipulated
To think something that never was
To have someone else control your mind

Memory loss is a dangerous thing
Especially when one takes advantage
To persuade you
To recognize one and to overlook another

There are such crooked people in this world
That take advantage

Memory loss is a hazardous thing where

people can take advantage
And cause more harm than good

When one forgets their remembrance
When one can depend on the people around
them
And when some can take advantage

The man in my dreams

Darkness fills my eyes
Finally sinking into subconscious
Finally to death

My Eyes open again
"Hey."
I see a man
Tall yet short
Eyes dark yet light
Smirk on his face
He is hiding
something from me
I'm dead right?
Surely not
I gave myself up on a silver platter
Yet here I am
Well and alive
With a mystery in my home

"You can't die
You haven't fulfilled your life
to the fullest
To the greatest

To the peak of the mountain
You just started
It may be bad
But don't you wanna know
what the future has in store
Don't you?"

"You can't."
"You can't just die yet
Life is a book
Dying now is
Writing a book
And never finishing
Leaving it on a cliffhanger
For everyone else to see in memorial
But yourself

Leaving the ends empty
Into complete darkness and dust
With abundant pages left

you can't
<u>You can't die just yet.</u>"

The words coming out of his mouth were
correct
That it's too early
I had just started the book
I can just leave it ending
Too bad, I had already had my chance

I was already dead
I was the man warning people
Trying to stop them
From making the same mistakes
like me
Trying to let them have a second chance
that's hard to get
At this game
That we call life

The clock

The clock ticks
tick..tock..tick..tock
Fear arises in my body
Fear of not having enough time
Fear of not being able to solve the perfects
and wrongings of this world

To fix every nerve ending

To make picture-perfect

The fear of having intellect inside of me
of what happens even in the far future

Or what happens in the far past

The events leading up to one another

The fear of not being able to solve

Time is a delicate thing
One event leads to another
Just a flick in the system can change

So much
Cause so much hurt and damage

Time is an intricacy

The fear of not being able to solve
Fix every perfect nerve ending

Fear rises inside of me

Times running out
I can't do anything
unless I want to cause doomsday

The past present and future
3 different things
All related to one another
A flick in the system
Can cause so many memories to decay
Can cause you to forget so much
Of your friends and family

Meddling with time is impossible
Like trying to mine iron with your bare
hands

Times running out
Tick...tock...tick...tock...
Fear remains inside of me
Tick..............

The wall

Sitting on your knees
Up against the wall
Pressed against your thoughts
Your brain can't take it all
The people know you exist
But pretend like they don't hear you at all
You're quiet and still feel so small
Though you're not really against the wall
Instead, you're in the middle of a shopping
mall
Surrounded by people
While onlooker's eyes watch you
As you suffer in your head all this long

Books: The new reality!

Books can be melancholy
Books can be sad
Can be happy
Books are filled with hundreds to thousands
of pages
All telling stories
Of the past
Present
Future
Whether fiction
Or truth
Books are lined with thousands of words

All books are the same
Leading us all to a never-ending fantasy
To another dimension
Where are lives are unique
Where we feel the greatest joys
Or the greatest sadness

At the end of the day
Once you turn that final page
It all disintegrates

It all goes away
It is just a stack of paper
Just a memory
A distraction

It's all a fantasy
To save yourself
From the wicked thoughts
Of this cruel little world

The garbage-filled city

The smell of the city got so bad
The smell of
Misery and sadness
The smell of agony and sabotage
The smell of revenge and pain
It smelled so bad
That you could stumble your words and
everyone would go mad

Once upon a time
In a world that seemed so far away
The city smelled like greatness and joy
Until the tiny oder
Got into everyone's head

The smell of the city got so bad
That everywhere you looked
Everyone was mad

The truth of reality

All my life
I've been trying to escape
Escape from the harsh reality
From the truth
From the damage
From the lies

But now as I lay down while the clock hits
12
I realize
I was just trying to escape myself.

Their "heartwarming" messages

They call you mean
Rude
Ruthless
Heartless
The worst

You like to think you don't care
About their harsh comments
Yet their words still burn into your skin

You ponder to yourself
Late in the night
That you're not mean
You're just in pain
But in time you realize
Maybe you are as heartless as they say you
are

Letting the hot words burn into your head
Turning you into a monster

Broken humans make heartless monsters

And heartless monsters make broken
humans

Leaving you trapped in a never-ending cycle
Of pain and regret

Good memories

It's funny
How a good memory
Can turn into a bad one
Instantly

How the tables can turn
Before you know it
Leaving you in dust

With your mind overheating
With the thoughts of all the things that went
wrong
Leaving you questioning
Why it was your fault
And not theirs
Even though it was their fault after all

The truth of love

The ones you love the most
Are the same ones
who will betray you
when you need them the most

The ones you love too much
Will kill you and leave you stranded
Alone

The ones who love you the most
Would fly you to the moon and back
And then stab you right in the back

The flood of denial

Denial
An act, a facade
To restrain the pain and loss
In a despair attempt to stray from the tide
Of ongoing conflict
To prevent the flood
Of acidic puddles of gloom

Island of doom

Anger
The feeling of hostility and frustration
Leaving you isolated and alone
Stranded on an island covered in glass
While you lose your shoes in the sand

Society's never happy, but are you?

To tall
To short
To fat
To skinny

Society's never happy.

Ugly face
Too much acne
lose some weight
Oh I thought you weren't hungry

Obese
Anorexic
Dysmorphic
Forget about the personality

To hairy
Small breasts
Sometimes I forget your human

Rude
Ugly

Loser
Dumb
Pull yourself together

Society's never happy
Going back and forth on a line
Asking for the opposite of one another
Till the end of time
To the shadows in the sky
Forgetting to ask the real question

"Are you even happy?"

Shipwreck of 12

I am human
Normal and to be criticized by everyone else
What no one cares or knows
Who lives the same life as 7.8 billion people
Who experiences emotions
like petals falling from a rose

As the clock hits 12
And my eyes close
My old friends toss me into the nothingness
of dirt and scorn
Where there is neither sense of joy nor love
But only betrayal and the shipwreck of
what's to come

Even the dearest that I loved left me alone
To wilt like an unwatered rose
And the ones who took care of me the most
Would rip me and tear me apart
Leaving me to wilt in self-pity on the side of
the road

So as the clock hits 12

And my eyes open
I smile
This time I toss my friends into a pit of
wilted roses
So I can feel love and joy again
So I can see a beautiful ship of what's to
come
Where there is no betrayal or heartbreak

A world where even the dearest I love the
most
Will let me be unique like a wild rose
Will not neglect me leaving me in the dark
For sadness to creep up on me
Eventually forcing me to wilt in self-pity

I am human
I am unique and will not be made fun of by
others
I am what I care and know of
I will not be made fun of for my hobbies,
laugh, or appearance
For I experience emotions like
The petals of a wild rose falling off

But time comes around and history repeats
As the clock hits 12
And I wake up from my dream
I say to myself "it was just never meant".

Take off

Run.
Run from the sharp blade of those who hurt
you
Run from the needy metal of those who
betrayed you
Run
Run Run RUN.
Run down the dark path till you can't feel
your legs no more
Run down the twisted curves of pavement
Run towards the light of the street lamp
Towards the feeling of comfort and safety
Keep running from the blade
In hopes your twisted past won't catch up to
you
Cause if you stop you better hope your past
has mercy on you.

Abandoned sky

Alone I stand
Body trembling and shaking
From the fall breeze that cuts my skin
Looking up at the shooting stars
I think to myself
That such a small flash of beauty
Is always to be seen and heard by the people
of this world
I watch as such a small thing can strike
wonders around the world
And strike wonders in hearts full of stone
Just how small words can strike love into a
heartbroken heart made of stone

Choose wisely

Slide down the risky path
Covered in sharp stones and bones
Take the risk and follow your dreams
If you are willing to achieve
The hardest of metal and stone

Or take the path covered in honey and
smooth stones
To follow your dreams in which you will
never achieve.

Bricks of diamonds

Don't cry
Don't waste your precious gems on those
Who caused you heartbreak and despair
Don't fall into the spiral of depression and
gloom
Over those who caused you the pain of a
thousand days
From the sun to the moon
Don't build walls around you and wonder
why they haven't come running back to you
Don't waste your tears flooding this earth

Instead, turn your heartbreak into joy and
plant them in your wounds
Waiting a thousand days and one day you
will have a wall of peace and tranquil

The shallow yard

With heart full of sorrow
I stand in my front yard
Hearing the crickets bust my ears
The raindrops breaking me into pieces
The grass burning my feet like hot tar
I stand there
Heart burning into my shirt
Filled with sorrow
Waiting for the person I loved the most to
come running back
Telling me that everything will be alright

Drowning of the lover

You've lost your humanity
Your empathy
Your love
And all your past

So why did you go fall in love
And ruin the friendship we'd had
Leaving me without a boat or anchor
To drown alone unpleasantly
While my screams are muffled by the deep
blue sea.

Brain decay

Day by day
Hour by hour
Minute by minute
Second by second
The ends of my mind begin to fray
Like overused clothes on a rainy day
Waiting to decay
And fly away into the windy breeze
On a terrible horrible no good day

I don't know what made my mind this way
And why it forced me to decay
But I do know who made it this way
And how they made me fray the fabric of
my brains away
On a terrible no good rainy day

Everything with nothing

She has everything
Everyone
And anything
She has people that love her
Friends who take care of her
Family that would do anything for her
People that would die for her
Yet she has nothing.

She has no one
Nobody
Zero
Cause "everything" is nothing
It's all an act
A facade
An illusion
Just to keep her sane while she stares at her
ceiling waiting for longing to return
And torture her till daylight
Till she breaks
And starts to imagine again

After all, she has "everything" doesn't she?

Mocking mirror

The man in the mirror stares at me
Mocking every movement and inch I take
Mocking all my past mistakes
Criticizing me for all the regretful choices I
make
Reminding me of all the tasteless words I
say

The man in the mirror stares at me
Making fun of me
Laughing his ass off at me
Waiting for a response out of me

The man in the mirror stares at me
Going quiet for the first time
Face full of shock and disbelief
By realizing he is me.

He's coming back?

Jack's not coming back
Jack's long gone the twisted rode
Riding his horse
Trying to find someone new
Don't try catching up to him
'Cus Jack's not coming back
He's riding along in the only horse you had
Don't ruin your feet trying to run to him
'Cus Jack's not coming back
Don't waste your tears on someone who
doesn't even like you
'Cus Jack's not coming back
Don't stress that he left you
'Cus Jack's not coming back
Be glad he's not coming back
'Cus he didn't deserve you
'Cus he's not coming back.

Intricacies of a simple thing

Red
The color of madness love and hatred
The sound of a man calling for war
The feeling of Chaos and destruction
The feeling of lust and love
The feeling of pure hatred and revenge
The color of a man going mad
The color of a man in love
The color of a man with hate running
through his veins
Red
A color that can describe many people and
many disruptions in this world.
R
E
D
The color for all
And the feeling of all

The lies we tell ourselves

People believe the unthinkable
The fact that they cannot achieve the
imaginable
That they cannot comprehend the believable
That they cannot pursue the despicable
People believe the lies they tell themselves
The negativity that they believe
Not the happiness that they can achieve
Not the accomplishments that will be
recognized
Not the compliments they receive
They see the recklessness they pursue
Not the happiness they begin
Not the life they grow
They let their minds rumble and glow
Thinking of the past of hate
Not the future of great
Rambling there minds
Diving into the ongoing feelings of hate
And distraught
Causing their negativity to take over their
brain
Eventually falling into a cliff full of pain

With joy and positivity holding their hand
out
Just out of reach
From the cliff of pain
Leaving people to be
To think the unthinkable

The misunderstood

Villains are framed to be the bad
To be the worst
To curse all of humanity
But villains aren't evil, bad, and up to no
good without a reason
Villains are created by the good
By the light
By the cool wind
Villains are born into the shadows because
the heroes consumed all the light
Villains are created from a hero's stupidity
From a hero's arrogance
From a selfish hero
Rude
And evil
Villains aren't bad for a reason
They are corrupted the by the real villains
The villains who pretend to be heroes but in
reality are cold-hearted and dark
Filled with arrogance and evil

You see, a true hero wouldn't have even
caused another villain

But a fake one with dark lusting evil
corrupting their heart take normal people
and turn them into monsters
Little do the heroes know that the villains
they face are their own creation
That they caused their own madness and
problems from their own creation
Because villains aren't evil
They are just corrupted by the heroes
Because a villain doesn't have their own
motives without a reason

Why do you think the villain's main target is
always the hero?
Not anyone else
Just people that come in their way from
beheading the hero and taking his throne and
crown
Because the throne and crown weren't the
heroes to begin with
It was stolen with the soul of another
It was stolen by a heartbreak of an innocent
civilian
Who turned to revenge and madness in
hopes it would solve all their problems

Too bad it won't because real heroes are hard
to find in this world
The only heroes here are corrupted
Making one villain to the next
Their own creation terrorizing them day to
night day by day.

So no, villains aren't bad people
They're just corrupted
By the so-called good.

The beauty of the terror

Life is a beautiful nightmare
Filled with love and tears
Pain and sickness
Joy and prosperity
Life will drag you up the walls
your mind spinning in circles
On beautifully carved walls with roses and
vines flowing out of them
While thorns bleed into your stomach as life
drags you all over them
The scent of love and lust filling your
nostrils
From the beautiful glowing roses
While the smell of copper and iron fills the
back of your head
From the painful blood that drips down your
spine
Eventually causing you to faint and fall on
your head
Gasping for air till you eventually flutter
your eyes open and realize you just fell off
your bed
With a sudden realization that

Life is like a beautiful nightmare
That twists and turns on a beautiful path
that's littered with glass instead of grass

Galaxy of hope

Echoes in my head
Of the galaxy calling me back
To my true home
Where life is filled with prosperity and joy
Not the fake life that I live filled with
injustice and crisis that crawls in the back of
my head
Filling me with negativity and pure sadness
I can still hear the echoes day by day as I
walk through the streets
Longing to go back
To the positivity and happiness
That filled my heart with love and the
promise of hope
As I walk through the streets with thousands
of thoughts on my mind
And the echoes to go home
To my past
My past memories
My past life
I miss the most important thing
My present

I miss the sounds of people passing by and
the screams of those behind me
I'm so caught up in negativity and the
memories of the past
That I miss the truck that hits me right in the
middle of the street going straight through
my bones
I miss the raw pain hitting me in the purest
way
I miss the feeling of positivity
I miss my past
I miss my memories
At what expense was I able to fill the hole of
longing in my heart with eternal peace

Complexity of life

High
Can mean a plethora of things
A person on something tall
An object close to the sky
A person climbing then looking down to
find people really small
A person on drugs
About to go do something that they'll regret
later
Whether that be now
Years from now
Or when there dead
Body in a coffin and all
From all the drugs they've consumed over
the years
During their lifetime
A simple thing to consume
That causes death damage and destruction
over time
High is such a simple word
Yet it can mean so many things
From a skyscraper to a coffin or a pile of
ashes

High
A word that can mean a plethora of things
Even relating to death

The irreversible

The past
Such an intricate thing
Something that cannot be reversed
Or gone back into
A moment in time where simple things that
happen can affect so much in the future
The past is so delicate that even a subtle
change can cause the destruction of
humanity
The past is happening as we breathe and we
talk about moments in time that we will
never be able to take back or experience
how it was then
The breaths of the air we take will never be
the same again
The words that come out of our mouths we
will never be able to change
That past is so delicate and intricate that
humans shouldn't be thinking about their
regrets and the things they've done
The past is the past something that cannot be
undone

So why think about it and waste your
present on regret when you can dream big
and believe in your future
Or even better yet spend more time with
those you love
The past is the past
An intricate thing that cannot be reversed or
undone
So stop regretting
And start believing

Numbered days

Death is when a person can say goodbye to
the world
Their heartbeat forever stopped
Their eyes will never witness the sun again
They will never see the beautiful
breathtaking sunrises and sunsets
They will never see the glimmering sunshine
and the admiring rain wept
Ever again.
So while you are on this earth
And in this land
Admire your every breath
And be thankful for every day you get to see
the sunrise and set
Even when things are tough
Remember that your days are numbered
And death is when it's your time to say
goodbye to the beauty's of the world

Inhuman v. Human

Emotions are an eloquent thing that pieces a
human together
Emotions are the glue to every factor and
challenge we face in the world
Love
Hunger
Sadness
Anger
All and more express our hearts and our
thoughts
Emotions allow us to enjoy the world
And the people around us
Emotions allow us to feel empathy and helps
to keep us in check when in the face of
ruthlessness
So next time you look cold-hearted
ruthlessness in the eyes
Remember your feelings
Your morality and your emotions
Because emotions may cause the world to be
a catastrophe however without them we
could have never truly experienced life

Emotions are an eloquent things that piece a
human together
causing us to be not as bad as we deem
ourselves to be

Blood pumping

Everyday
Every minute
Every second
Your heart beats
Thump.....Thump
Pumping blood keeping you alive every day
Making sure you have a chance to live
To see the sky every day
And to see the sunrise and fall
However
The heart is special
An intricate thing
The heart tells you the things you couldn't
even think of
Things you wouldn't even imagine
It tells you the things you think
subconsciously
The things you wouldn't dare to say out loud
The things you refuse to express
Your heart guides you through different
paths
Some good
Some bad

And sometimes you don't even know it
Thump...Thump...Thump
When your heart slows down or speeds up
It's telling you a message
A meaning
A cause
But only if you pay close attention
Your heart beats faster
When you're scared
When you're in love
When you work till you can't feel yourself
anymore
When you're anxious
When you're thrilled
When you cry
Your heart tells you things you wouldn't
even recognize

Everyday
Every minute
Every second
Your heart beats
Telling you the secrets of your own body
But you only learn the true messages

If you pay close attention to the thing we all
have inside of us
Everyday
Every minute
Every second
Your heart beats
So listen to it
And maybe you'll learn something new
Or learn the obvious in front of you
Thump.....

½ of a heart

Never work halfheartedly
Work with your full potential
Because sometimes the outrageous is
possible
If you don't work with all your might you
may regret the things you haven't done
You may miss opportunities you wanted to
come
You may miss the right times
you could have achieved the unthinkable
You can't decide your fate
But you can work with your heart
And work with your full potential
Never work halfheartedly
Because the inevitable is possible
And you may regret not working to your
fullest
Never work halfheartedly
Because you may just miss the best
opportunity life has to offer

Why not?

If you can stop a heart from breaking then
why not help
If you could save a man from failing then
why not help
If you could help a poor man then why not
help
If you can do so much then why not help
Why be selfish and ignorant of the people
around you
If you have the power to help
Why be ignorant and selfish when you can
help
If you can save at least one life
Then why not help
Why be selfish
Instead of selfless

It's too early

It's never too late to do something
It's never too late to turn around and fix
your life
It's never too late to turn a man's life upside
down
It's never about too late
It's always about your laziness
There's never a limit to what you can do
What you hope to achieve
What you can't do
What you wish to do
There is no such thing as "too late"
It's always about you
It's about what you want to do
Because there is no limit in life
It's never too late
It's just because you believe you are not
capable
But the truth is a man is capable of anything
but only if they strive
So no there is never a time that it is too late
It's just about you
And what you chose to do

Tough planet

The world is a beautiful nightmare
Filled with chaos and elegance
Filled with charm and violence
Filled with love and hatred
It takes a strong man to see the whole world
from the inside out and appreciate its
nightmare filled glory

Duality of a face

Friends
Family
Lovers
Can all be beautiful kind pretty
Delightful and eloquent on the outside
But can be filled with hatred and jealousy on
the inside
So it's okay to walk away from them
sometimes
And give yourself a peaceful mind
It may hurt
But that's what you have to do because of
what they gave in return for your care and
affectionate words
Friends
Family
Lovers
Can all be beautiful kind
Delightful and eloquent on the outside
But can be filled with hatred and jealousy on
the inside
So it's okay to walk away from them
sometimes

Inevitable experience

Remember this
Not everything is permanent
Life may have its twists and turns
But it will always keep going
No matter how much sadness or anger you
feel
It will never be there forever
At one point whether that be years or days
Your feeling will disintegrate
Because in life nothing
And I mean nothing
Is permanent

You are still operating

Live in the moment
Because you may never know when you
forget that moment
Enjoy the laughter
Experience the pain
Embrace the freedom
Thrive in the joy
Live your life how you want to live it
Don't hold things off for other times
Live in the moment
And be free in it
Because you may never know when the
clocks come tumbling down
And you forget that very moment.

Look in a mirror

Sometimes you may be the cause of your
own problems
Your own enemy
And you may not even know it
Diminishing yourself day by day
Causing your own stress and problems
You need to re-evaluate yourself
Learn more about the you inside
In order to understand yourself and your
difficulties
In order to recognize the enemy in you
And to recognize your other thoughts and
emotions
Imagine the south star instead of the north
A world where everything was opposite
In order to re-evaluate your mind and
thoughts
Imagine a world where opposites don't
attract
Because to understand the true enemy in you
You must take measures in which you would
never expect

Foreground middle ground background

Nobody is in the background
Everybody is the background
To a world filled with human emotions
Humans are just a small part of the world
Just the background of millions of things
Nobody is ever in the background or the side
character
Everyone is the background
Being the main character in their lives
Nobody is in the background
Everyone and everybody is the background

Monsters under our bed

We create our own monsters
Building them and tearing them apart with
our own hands and claws
Making them like a piece of art
With all our deepest fears and insecurities
Shaping our monsters to know us so they
know how to haunt us day and night
Carving every insecurity and every tiny little
detail in our monsters
Shaping them into perfection
With our bare hands and claws
With the brains skin and veins of sculptures
that look like fine art
We put every little detail into our monsters
carving them day and night
Just so they know how to tear us apart
We are our own monsters

2% remaining

You don't have to try to please everyone
It's not your job to spend your life's
emotions and your health
on someone else
like a slow depleting battery
With no charger to be found.

Deterioration of forever

Forever
Maybe a minute or a second
Sometimes may last forever
Forever is a versatile word that's overused in
common conversation
So your love or your hope and your joy may
not last forever
Because human emotions can go just so long
without deterioration
Just like our bodies as we grow old
Nothing lasts forever
But as long as you breathe and live
To you forever can mean anything and
everything
Even if your forever and joy last for a split
second
It can change the world and turn your heart
upside down
Nothing will ever last forever but your
words and thoughts can
Because forever doesn't have to mean
eternity

Forever can be seconds minutes hours days
and even years
Depending on your thoughts and hope
But no matter how long it lasts forever can
strike a match of hope in your heart and
maybe even a match of despair
Turning and changing your world upside
down for the better or worse
Forever
Maybe a minute or a second
And will last forever depending on your
hope and despair

Forever: an amount of time your human
mind chooses

Quarks

Enjoy the little things
Because you never know when it can all end
with a snap
From the ground, you are on to the nature
around us
Enjoy everything
No matter how small
Because one the day you will never have a
chance to see the earth how it was ever
again
So enjoy the little things from the smallest
grain of sand to the tallest skyscraper on
earth
Because you never know when it can all end
in a snap.

Natural drugs

Stress is a necessity in life
Without it you would have no motivation
Or drive to do the simplest
Things in life
However that doesn't mean to cloud your
world and mind with it
Only use stress in the most extreme places
In order to feel a rush of drive and
motivation
But don't spend your entire life living with it
And letting stress fog up your brain like an
addictive drug

New and improved

Sometimes the simplest of things can make
you feel like a brand new person
Just treating yourself right can cause your
distress to go away
And make you feel like you're worth a
million bucks
Just the simplest actions
Just a smile
Can cause your world to turn upside down
Causing your frown to turn into a face full
of joy
Sometimes the simplest things can make you
feel like a brand new person.

A fresh bouquet

Bells of Ireland for *luck….*
Yellow carnations for *Rejection*
Broom for *humility*
Aloe for *grief*
Bird's-foot trefoil for *revenge*
Peony for *anger*
Narcissus for *selfishness*
Black Tulip for *power*
Tansy for *war*
Black Dahlia for *betrayal*
Wormwood for *absence*
Yarrow for *healing*
Orange tulip for *understanding*
Yarrow for *healing*
White tulips for *forgiveness.*

The opposites

You must go through the sorrow pain and
the sickness
In order to reach the peace and tranquility
that lies ahead of you
You must climb the mountains of terror
In order to reach for the stars of beauty
You must be the ugly
In order to be the perfection
You must go through the bad
In order to reach for the good
That lies ahead waiting for you till time ends

Children's play

A merry go round
Spinning around and round
Over and over
While you can hear the joy and laughter of
kids smiles spread
Infecting more and more people
Over the course of childhood joy
Just how violence and revenge spins
Over and over
Spinning around and round
While you can see the pain anger and
sickness of people's hearts spread
Infecting more and more people
Over the course of revenge

Class begins

I can hear the sighs of my classmates
Translating into pressure
And chaos
Causing a disruption into the atmosphere
A class filled with stress
Looking up at the ticking clock
Waiting for the day to end

No once mores

You only live once
So what's there to live without fulfilling
your wildest of dreams
What's there to live if you can't have fun
Why waste your precious life rotting away
in a chair when you can be out and about
having fun
A life is a delicacy
You only live once
So before it ends
Live to your fullest potential
And achieve the things you never knew you
could achieve

First steps

Waking up with the sun blazing fire on you
With your eyes fluttering open to the
lightness that surrounds you
Moving the hefty covers off your body
slowly and rationally
Taking a deep breath and moving your body
slowly up off the bed
As soon as your feet touch the soft warm
ground
You take your first steps of the day
Pondering in what will to come
Wondering if you'll come back to the very
bed you slept on
With joy and prosper in your heart
Or fire and rage
Or thunder and sadness

Human anatomy

The brain
Most powerful organ
Controls your every being
Controls your every expression
Your every word
Every thought
Memory
Hunger
Temperature
Vison
Breathing
Yet we blame our hearts
Whenever we experience
The
Pain
Loss
Suffering
Greed
Because we feel as if a piece of our heart has
been torn up and played around with
Like a dog's chew toy
Waiting to be used over and over again
We never blame our brains

Never blame ourselves
For problems that may have been caused by
our own
Pain
Loss
Suffering
Greed
The brain is the most powerful organ of the
body
It helps you to express your entire life and
the choices you make along with it

Veracious

Madman
Madman
Madman
Madman
Is what they all call me
But it's not my fault they can't see through
the eyes of truth
That they can't see
See
See
See
The glorious great all beautiful truth that lies
ahead of them
They blame me
Me
Me
ME
Can you believe it they blame poor old me
Starting I sell lies and myths
They all blame me
Call me a mad men
Even though I am just like them
I am them

Them
Them
Them
Except I don't look the truth in the eye and
chose to deny it
Deny
Deny
DENY IT
Madman
Madman
Madman
Madman
Is what they all call me
But it's not my fault they can't see through
the eyes of truth
Madman
Madman
Madman
Is what they all call me
But it's not my fault I recognize the truth
they refuse to acknowledge
I may be a madman but one thing I may not
be is someone who denies the painfully
obvious truth
That lies straight in their field of vision

Madman
Madman
Madman
Madman
Is what they all call me
But it's not my fault they can't see through
the eyes of truth.

The broken line

Alone in her house
The women sat
Holding a telephone in her bare hands
Wondering through the sound of the static
silence
What words
Could rekindle the flame of love
Covered in dust
With her drooping eyes
Carrying the pressure of her broken heart
With pain and sickness tearing it apart

The women sat down
All night
Pondering on what to say
To relight the flame
Till the clock hit 12
Alarming her that she had nothing to say
Not saying a single sentence remaining
So she cut the line
Forever extinguishing the flame of love
That perished into ashes
On a broken line at midnight

To you….
My dear reader who got to see all the pieces
of a flame that got extinguished on
A broken line at midnight

A broken line at midnight
Ashes of the broken line forever tarnished
turned into a collection of poems

By: Ayaana Noman

Farewell, my reader.